counting

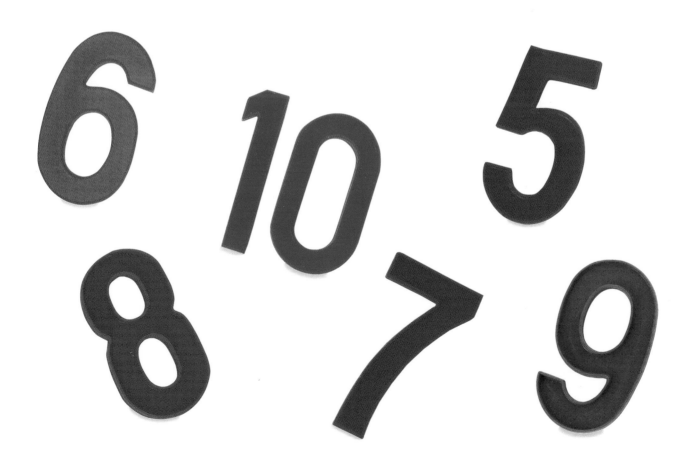

LOOK & LEARN

counting

1 2 3 4

a first point & say book

southwater

One to five

Can you find...

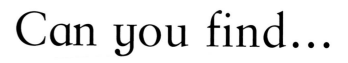

1 wooden rocking horse

3 pretty plants

2 candy sticks

5 floating feathers

4 cuddly teddy bears

2 playful puppies

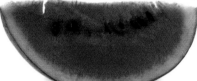

5 juicy
watermelon
slices

1 smiling baby

4 crunchy apples

Six to ten

Can you find...

6 toy cars

10 different hats

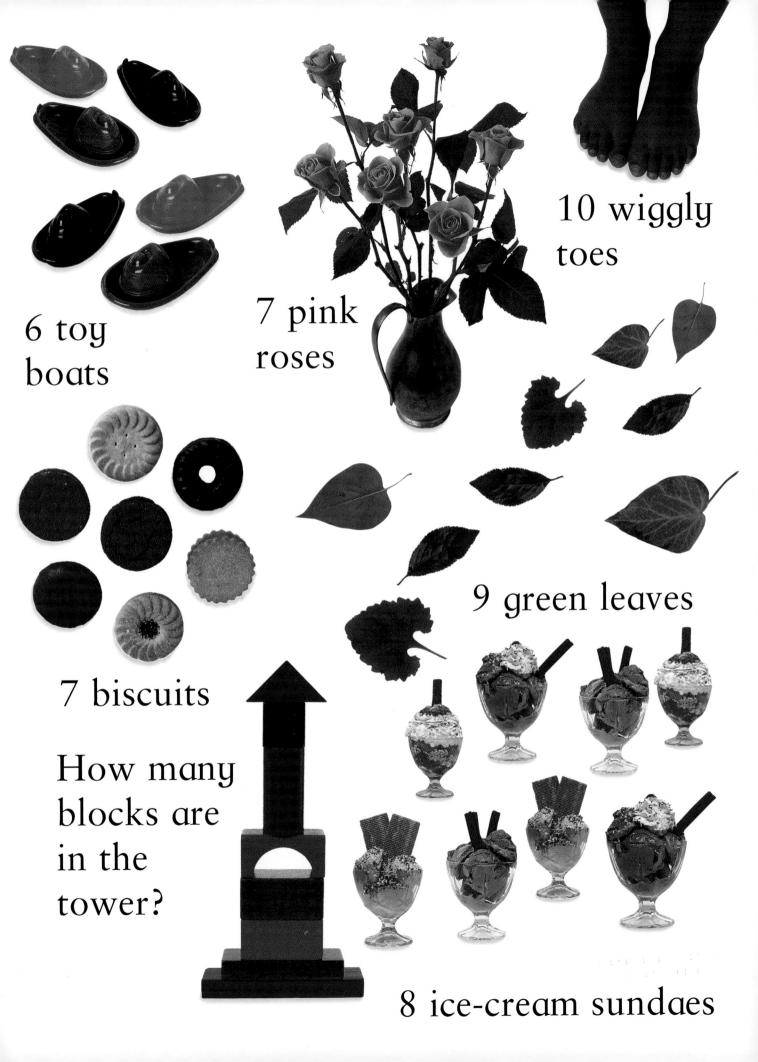

6 toy boats

7 pink roses

10 wiggly toes

7 biscuits

9 green leaves

How many blocks are in the tower?

8 ice-cream sundaes

Counting up to 20

Can you count 20 teddy bears?

Counting down

 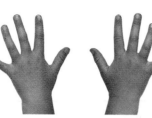

Sometimes you have to count down from 10 to 1.

When would you do this?

 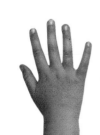 

Lift off!

Look at
the Space
shuttle...

...flying
into
Space!

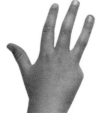 

Numbers everywhere

Almost everywhere you look there are numbers.

dominoes

price tags

49p

clown clock

football shirt

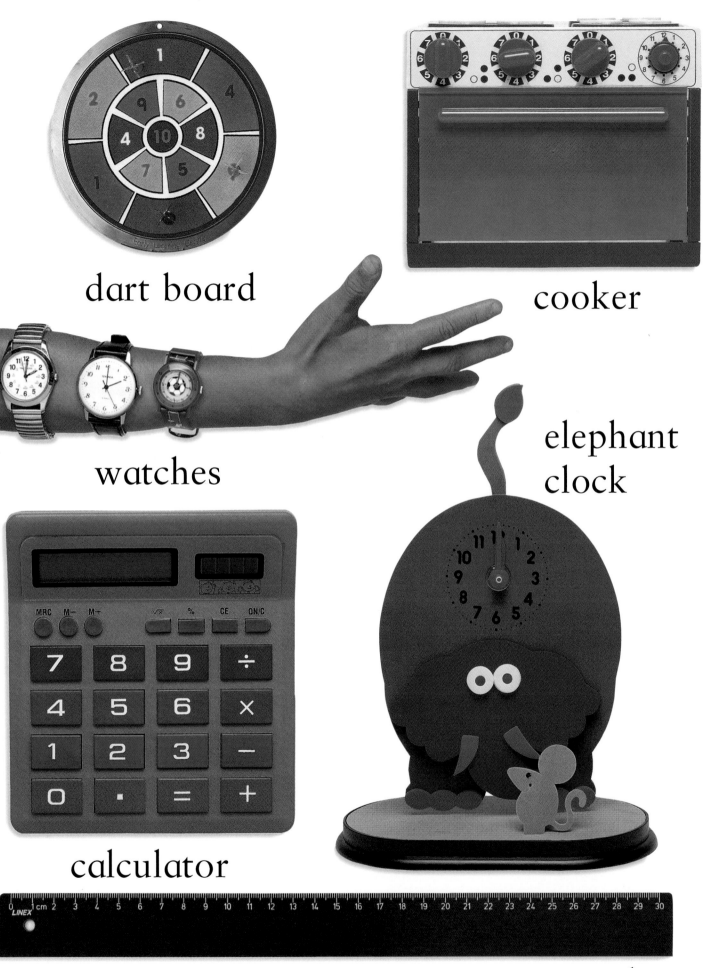

dart board

cooker

watches

elephant
clock

calculator

ruler

How many?

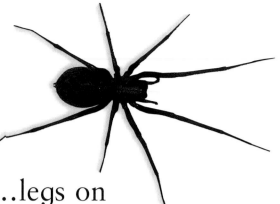

...legs on a spider?

You can count all sorts of things. How many...

...animals on a trailer?

...spots on the dice?

...flowers in a window box?

…wheels on a bicycle?

…bricks in a tower?

…lollies in a row?

…bobbles on the gloves?

…blocks on a bulldozer?

Animal numbers

Animals are fun to count.

3 slimy snails

1 timid rabbit

10 marching ants

5 golden hamsters

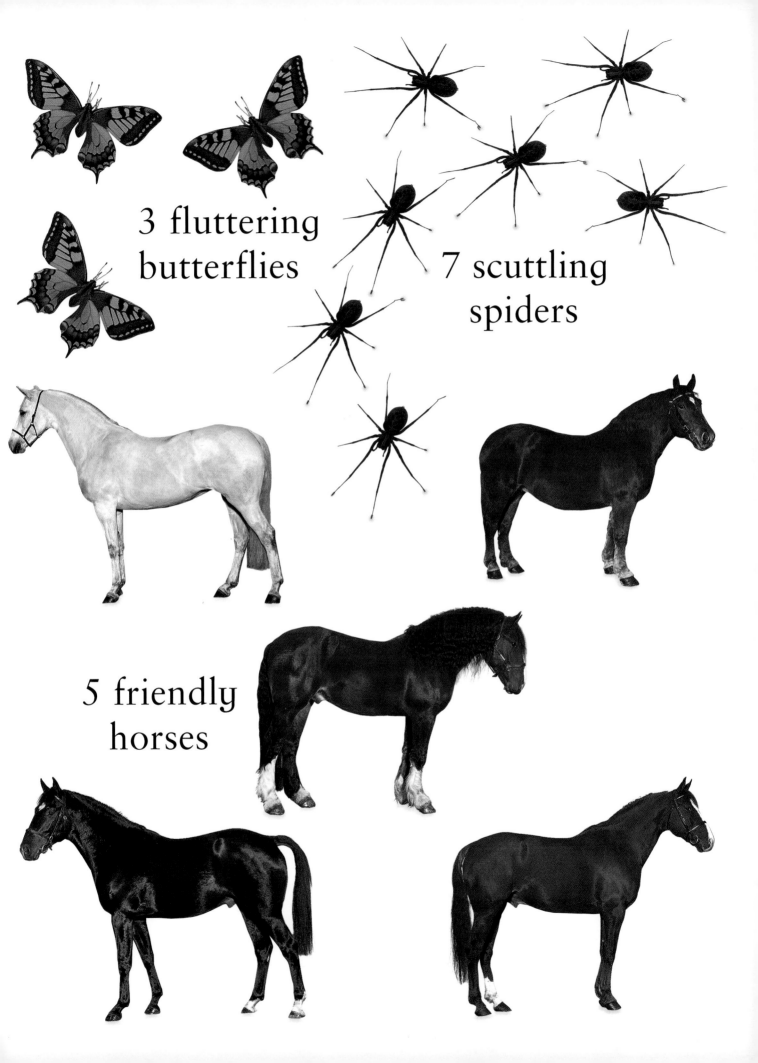

3 fluttering
butterflies

7 scuttling
spiders

5 friendly
horses

Are there enough?

Count to see if there are the same number of...

...carrots for the rabbits

...spoons for the ice creams

...fairy cakes and cherries

...saucers of milk for the kittens

...flowers
for the
butterflies

Add it up

+
=

+ means add together

= means equals, or how many altogether

Count two puppies.

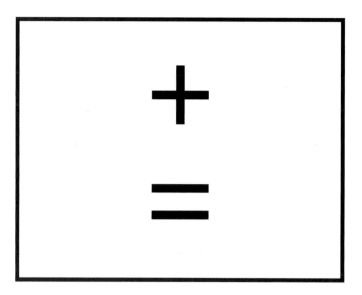

+

Count three spaniels.

+

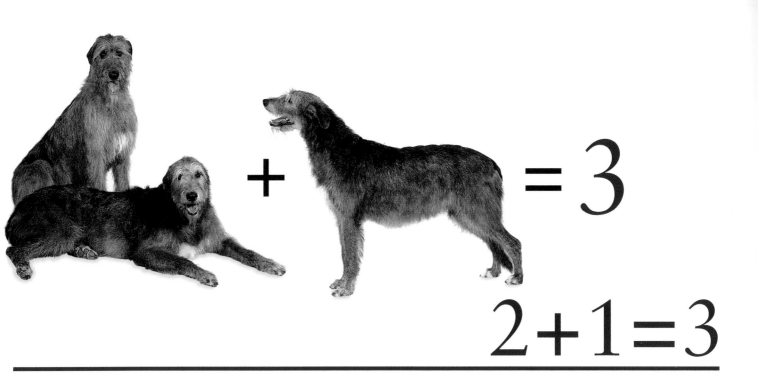

$+$ $= 3$

$2+1=3$

Add two more.

$=$ How many altogether?

$2+2=4$

Add three more.

$=$ How many altogether?

$3+3=6$

Add some more

+ means add

= means equals

Count these things and add them together. Can you write the sums?

Count five bath soaps.

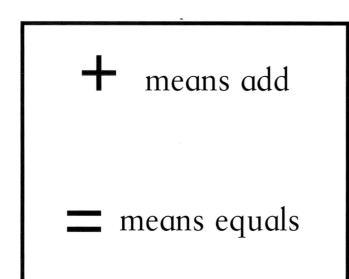
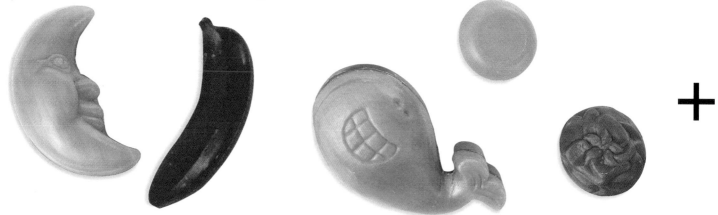

+

Count six bath whales.

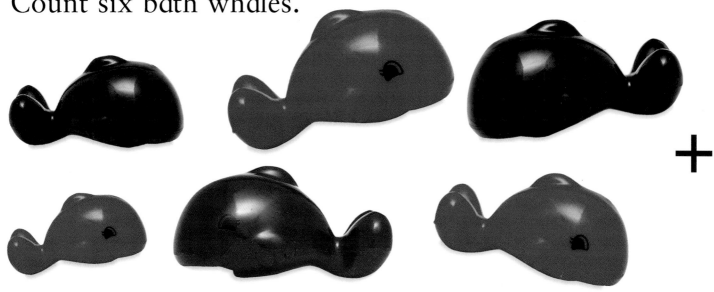

+

Count two
toy boats.

Add four more.

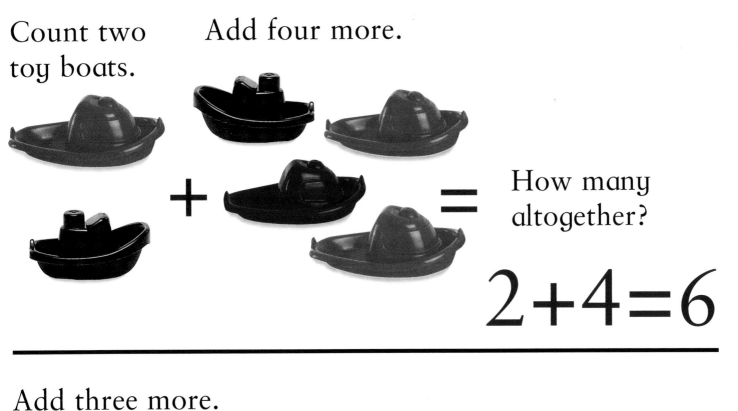

+

=

How many
altogether?

$$2+4=6$$

Add three more.

=

How many
altogether?

$$5+3=8$$

Add three more.

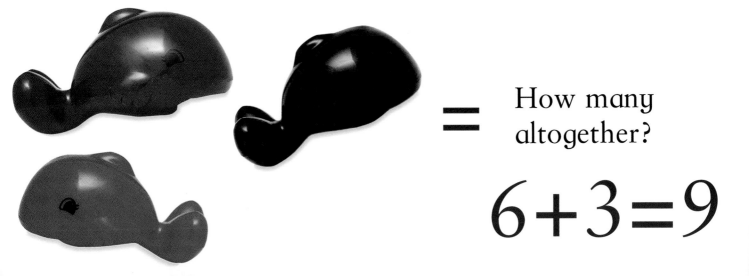

=

How many
altogether?

$$6+3=9$$

Take it away

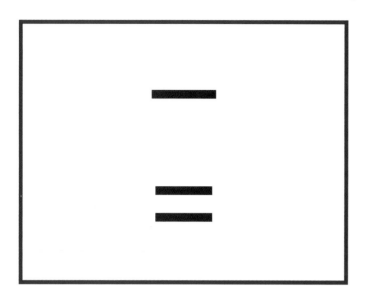

– means take away

= means equals,
or how many
altogether

Count four cats in collars.

Count four cats washing.

$$3-1=2$$

Two crawl away.   How many are left?

$$4-2=2$$

One goes away.   How many cats are left?

$$4-1=3$$

Going, going, gone

—	means take away
=	means equals

Taking things away means there are fewer things left in the end.

Count five trucks.

Count four children on wheels.

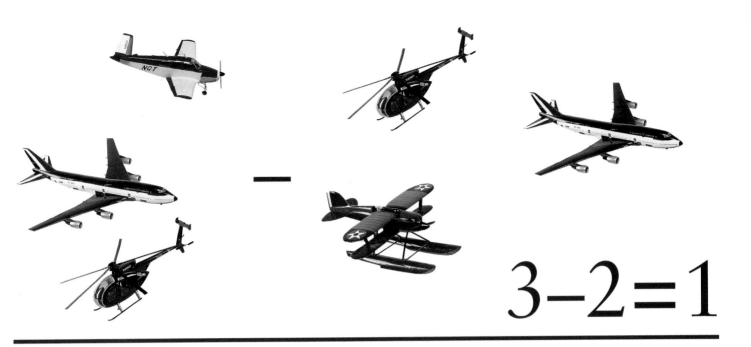

$$3-2=1$$

Take one away.   How many are left?

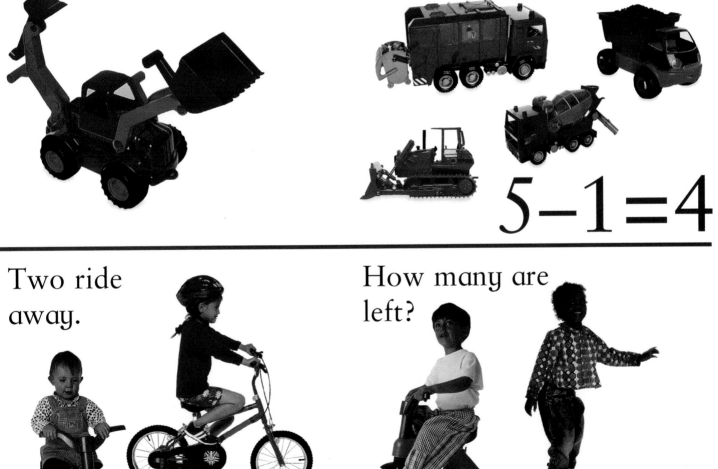

$$5-1=4$$

Two ride away.   How many are left?

$$4-2=2$$

Great big numbers

Now you can count some really big numbers. Count...

...30 squares

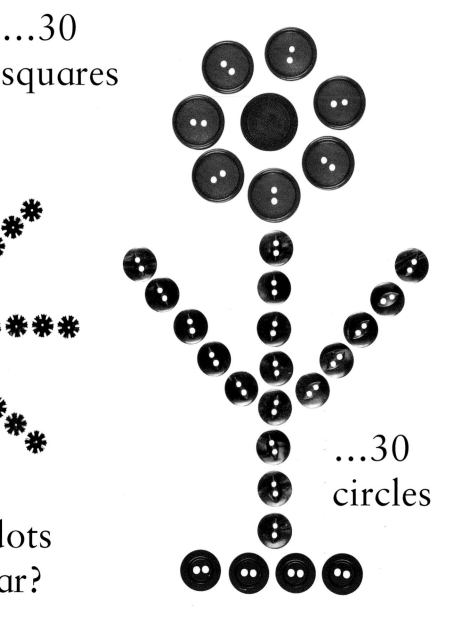

...30 circles

How many dots are in the star?

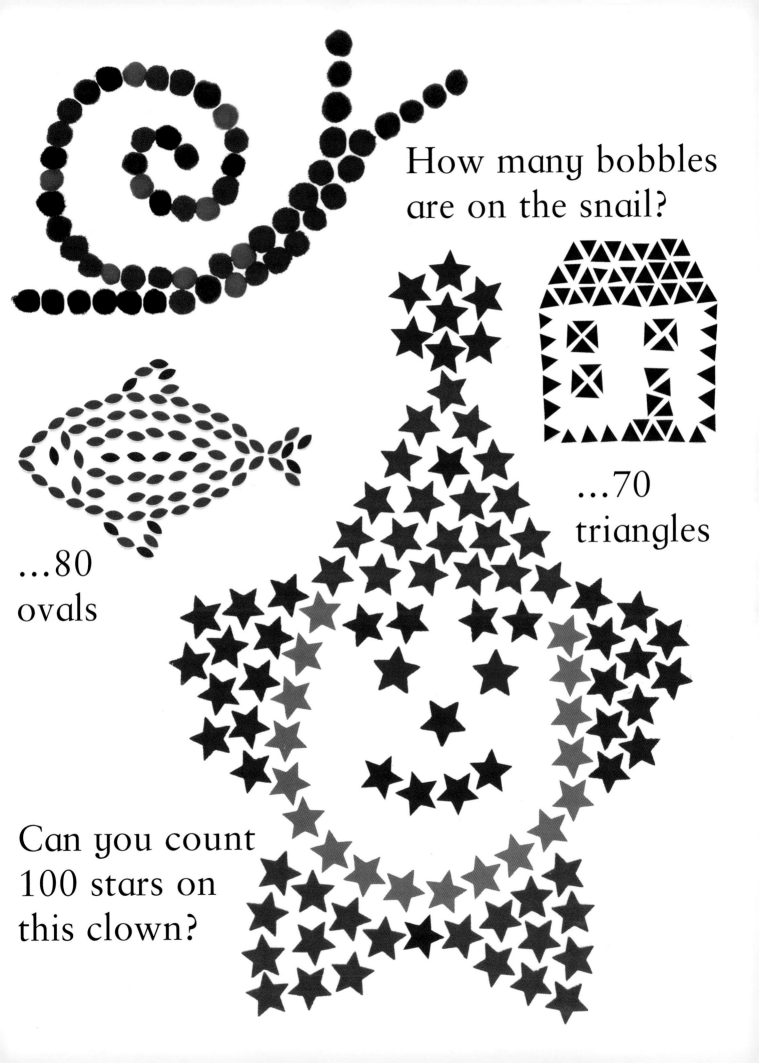

How many bobbles
are on the snail?

...70
triangles

...80
ovals

Can you count
100 stars on
this clown?

Can you count...

6 blue cars?

8 ice-cream sundaes?

3 juicy
strawberries?

1 clown
clock?

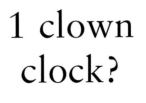

This edition is published by Southwater

Southwater is an imprint of
Anness Publishing Ltd
Hermes House
88–89 Blackfriars Road
London SE1 8HA
tel. 020 7401 2077
fax 020 7633 9499

Distributed in the UK by
The Manning Partnership
251–253 London Road East
Batheaston
Bath BA1 7RL
tel. 01225 852 727
fax 01225 852 852

Distributed in the USA by
National Books Network
4720 Boston Way
Lanhan
MD 20706
tel. 301 459 3366
fax 301 459 1705

Distributed in Australia by
Sandstone Publishing
Unit 1, 360 Norton Street
Leichhardt
New South Wales 2040
tel. 02 9560 7888
fax 02 9560 7488

Publisher: Joanna Lorenz
Managing Editor, Children's Books: Gilly Cameron Cooper
Project Editor: Belinda Weber   Designer: Sandra Marks at Axis Design
Photographers: John Freeman and Lucy Tizard

The publishers would like to thank the following children for modelling for this series of books: Rosie
Anness, Harriet Bartholomew, Jonathan Bartholomew, Daisy Bartlett, Karl Bolger, Lee Bolger, Caspian
Broad, Andrew Brown, April Cain, Freddy Cassford, Milo Clare, Tayah Ettienne, Matthew Ferguson,
Africa George, Safari George, Saffron George, Jamie Grant, Zoe Harrison, Jack Harvey-Holt, Max
Harvey-Holt, Erin Hoel, Alice Jenkins, Kathleen Jenkins, Amber McLaren, Rebekah Murrell, Nell
Nixon, Tiffani Ogilvie, Philip Quach, Giovanni Sipiano, Giuseppe Sipiano.

Previously published as part of a larger compendium, *Point and Say: Playschool Fun*